ANIMAL SAFARI

Platypuses

by Megan Borgert-Spaniol

BELLWETHER MEDIA • MINNEAPOLIS, MN

Note to Librarians, Teachers, and Parents:

Blastoff! Readers are carefully developed by literacy experts and combine standards-based content with developmentally appropriate text.

Level 1 provides the most support through repetition of high-frequency words, light text, predictable sentence patterns, and strong visual support.

Level 2 offers early readers a bit more challenge through varied simple sentences, increased text load, and less repetition of high-frequency words.

Level 3 advances early-fluent readers toward fluency through increased text and concept load, less reliance on visuals, longer sentences, and more literary language.

Level 4 builds reading stamina by providing more text per page, increased use of punctuation, greater variation in sentence patterns, and increasingly challenging vocabulary.

Level 5 encourages children to move from "learning to read" to "reading to learn" by providing even more text, varied writing styles, and less familiar topics.

Whichever book is right for your reader, Blastoff! Readers are the perfect books to build confidence and encourage a love of reading that will last a lifetime!

This edition first published in 2016 by Bellwether Media, Inc.

No part of this publication may be reproduced in whole or in part without written permission of the publisher. For information regarding permission, write to Bellwether Media, Inc., Attention: Permissions Department, 5357 Penn Avenue South, Minneapolis, MN 55419.

Library of Congress Cataloging-in-Publication Data

Borgert-Spaniol, Megan, 1989- author.
  Platypuses / by Megan Borgert-Spaniol.
    pages cm. – (Blastoff! Readers. Animal Safari)
  Summary: "Developed by literacy experts for students in kindergarten through grade three, this book introduces platypuses to young readers through leveled text and related photos"– Provided by publisher.
  Audience: Ages 5-8
  Audience: K to grade 3
  Includes bibliographical references and index.
  ISBN 978-1-62617-212-8 (hardcover: alk. paper)
  1. Platypus–Juvenile literature. I. Title. II. Series: Blastoff! readers. 1, Animal safari.
  QL737.M72B67 2016
  599.2'9-dc23
                                                    2015004210

Printed in the United States of America, North Mankato, MN.

Contents

What Are Platypuses?

Platypuses are **mammals**. They live near lakes, rivers, and streams.

Platypuses rest in **burrows** during the day. They swim at night.

Webbed feet and flat tails help them move through water. Thick fur keeps them warm.

webbed feet

Bottom Feeders

Platypuses are **bottom feeders**. They feel for **prey** with their **bills**.

They scoop up
shellfish, worms,
and **insects**.
They swim to the
surface to eat.

Platypuses have no teeth. They crush food with rough pads in their mouths.

Eggs to Babies

A female lays two soft eggs in her burrow. Her body keeps them warm.

Baby platypuses **hatch** 10 days later. Each is the size of a jelly bean.

The babies drink mom's milk for several months. Then they are ready to hunt. To the water!

Glossary

bills—the smooth, rubber-like outer parts of the mouths of platypuses

bottom feeders—animals that search for food along the bottom of a body of water

burrows—holes or tunnels that some animals dig in the ground

hatch—to break out of an egg

insects—small animals with six legs and hard outer bodies; insect bodies are divided into three parts.

mammals—warm-blooded animals that have backbones and feed their young milk

prey—animals that are hunted by other animals for food

shellfish—animals that live in water and have shells; shrimp, clams, and crabs are types of shellfish.

surface—the top of a body of water

webbed feet—feet with thin skin that connects the toes

To Learn More

AT THE LIBRARY

Clarke, Ginjer L. *Platypus!* New York, N.Y.: Random House, 2004.

Collard, Sneed B. *Platypus, Probably.* Watertown, Mass.: Charlesbridge, 2005.

Kras, Sara Louise. *Platypuses.* Mankato, Minn.: Capstone Press, 2010.

ON THE WEB

Learning more about platypuses is as easy as 1, 2, 3.

1. Go to www.factsurfer.com.

2. Enter "platypuses" into the search box.

3. Click the "Surf" button and you will see a list of related web sites.

With factsurfer.com, finding more information is just a click away.

Index

The images in this book are reproduced through the courtesy of: manwithacamera.
com.au/ Alamy, front cover; worldswildlifewonders, p. 5; Peter Scoones/ Science
Source, p. 7; David Watts/ Visuals Unlimited/ Corbis, p. 9; Universal Images Group/
SuperStock, p. 11; D. Parer & E. Parer-Cook/ Newscom, p. 13 (top); Aleksey Stemmer,
p. 13 (bottom left); waw ritto, p. 13 (bottom center); Photo Fun, p. 13 (bottom right);
Lacz, Gerard/ Animals Animals, p. 15; Dave Watts/ Alamy, p. 17; Jason Edwards/
National Geographic Creative, p. 19; Laura Romin & Larry Dalton/ Alamy, p. 21
(top); Photodigitaal.nl, p. 21 (bottom).